M000033269

OBAMAMANIA!

THE ENGLISH LANGUAGE, BARACKAFIED

THE EDITORS OF **Slate**

EDITED BY CHRIS WILSON

A FIRESIDE BOOK

PUBLISHED BY SIMON & SCHUSTER

NEW YORK   LONDON   TORONTO   SYDNEY

Fireside
A Division of Simon & Schuster, Inc.
1230 Avenue of the Americas
New York, NY 10020

Copyright © 2008 *Slate*

All rights reserved, including the right to reproduce this book or portions thereof in any form whatsoever.
For information address Fireside Subsidiary Rights Department, 1230 Avenue of the Americas, New York, NY 10020.

First Fireside trade paperback edition June 2008

FIRESIDE and colophon are registered trademarks of Simon & Schuster, Inc.

For information about special discounts for bulk purchases,
please contact Simon & Schuster Special Sales at 1-800-456-6798 or business@simonandschuster.com.

Designed by Ruth Lee-Mui

Manufactured in the United States of America

1   3   5   7   9   10   8   6   4   2

Library of Congress Cataloging-in-Publication Data
Obamamania! : the English language, Barackafied / the editors of Slate.—1st Fireside trade pbk. ed.
p.   cm.
"A Fireside book."
1. Obama, Barack—Humor. 2. Vocabulary—Humor I. Slate (Redmond, Wash.)
PN6231.O22O23 2008
428.102'07—dc22   2008020021

ISBN-13: 978-1-4165-9649-3
ISBN-10: 1-4165-9649-6

FOREWORD

On a Tuesday night in Boston, in July 2004, Barack Obama took the stage at the Democratic National Convention to introduce himself to America. At the top of the agenda: that funny assemblage of *b*'s and *a*'s that he called a name.

His parents, he said, "would give me an African name, Barack, or 'blessed,' believing that in a tolerant America, your name is no barrier to success."

Looking back, it's safe to say that Barack Obama's name has been anything but a barrier in his bid for the presidency of the United States of America. Quite the opposite. The brightest minds of

Madison Avenue would be hard-pressed to gin up a better brand name for Obama's narrative of the bounty of America's melting pot. Even his middle name, Hussein, once shorthand for evil incarnate in the Bush administration's quixotic forays into war, has found a place in his message of reconciliation to move beyond the tired politics of xenophobia. Through no particular effort of his own, Barack Obama's name began its offensive on the American lexicon.

The name Barack Obama is also, incidentally, a gift from above for those of us who doodle anagrams on our lunch breaks. It is almost 50 percent vowels—bad for anagrams, actually, but perfect for arranged marriages with other words that describe his improbable candidacy. The English language, arguably Obama's greatest weapon in his bid for the presidency, is ripe for Obamafication.

In that spirit, *Slate* presents *Obamamania!*, more than one hundred words that have been retrofitted with Obama's moniker to create a new vocabulary for this unusual campaign. Some of them you have no doubt heard before, from *Obamenon* to *Barackstar*. Others, we would wager, are new to this volume. Try *deus ex Barachina* on for size, and don't forget to taste our chef's special, the *Baratwurst*.

This book began as an idle e-mail discussion among *Slate* writers who had noticed more and more Obamaisms cropping up in this campaign. Once we realized that there were so many possibilities, we compiled the best of them into a feature on *Slate* and invited readers to submit their own words and definitions. Great words continue to roll in daily. The definitions in this book are a combination of our original offerings and these submissions, many of which have not previously been published.

We hope readers find these words and definitions entertaining. There are, after all, worse ways in this interminable election to keep yourself Barackupied.

PEOPLE

Baractogenarian

(buh-ROK-tuh-juh-NAIR-ee-uhn) *n.*

An Obama supporter over the age of twenty.

Barackiosaurus

(buh-RAK-ee-uh-SAWR-uhs) *n.*

Anyone born before 1960, in the eyes of an Obama evangelist. *See also:* BARACTOGENARIAN.

"I know it's kind of lame to break up with you on Valentine's Day. And on the Internet to boot. But it's also kind of ironic. And that's what I need to tell you. As an ironic, contrarian, so-hip-it-hurts Gen Xer, I just can't love you anymore. I can't like you because . . . because, well, everyone else does. And suddenly supporting you just seems *soooo* last week."

Slate's **Dahlia Lithwick**, "Letter from a young, hip, cynical former Obamamaniac," February 14, 2008

Obahmadinejad
(oh-bah-mah-DIH-nee-zhahd) *n.*

The field coordinator for the Obama campaign's Tehran office.

Obamaton
(oh-BAH-muh-ton) *n.*

Any mechanical Obama supporter constructed to act as if by its own motivation. *See also:* OBOMBIES (p. 5).

Obombies

(oh-BOM-bees) *n.*

Supporters who, though expressing unwavering support for Barack Obama, cannot name a single one of his policies.

> While they make poor debaters, the Obombies' contagious ability to create more Obombies has proven useful in filling arenas.

Obamateur

(oh-BOM-uh-choor) *n*.

A person who gives rousing stump speeches for pleasure rather than financial benefit.

Obamazon

(oh-BAH-muh-zon) *n*.

1. A passionate female Obama supporter. **2.** An online bookseller that stocks only two books, *The Audacity of Hope* and *Dreams from My Father*.

Obama-GYN

(oh-BAH-mah gee-wahy-ehn) *n.*

An expert on the female body's response to Obama.

Obamanatrix

(oh-bom-uh-NEY-triks) *n.*

A person who has incorporated Obama Girl into her sexual fantasies.

Obombre

(oh-BOM-brey) *n.*

A Spanish-speaking male who supports Obama.

Obamafioso

(oh-bah-mah-fee-OH-soh) *n.*

An Obama supporter who resorts to extortion and blackmail to get Barack Obama elected. *See also:* BARACKETEERING (p. 98).

"And everywhere I'd go, I'd get two questions. First they'd ask, 'Where'd you get that funny name, Barack Obama?' Because people just couldn't pronounce it. They'd call me 'Alabama,' or they'd call me 'Yo Mama.' And I'd tell them that my father was from Kenya, and that's where I got my name. And my mother was from Kansas, and that's where I got my accent from."

Barack Obama in a speech to the California State Democratic Convention, April 28, 2007

Obamrade
(oh-BOM-rad) *n.*

A person who attempts to reconcile the teachings of Barack Obama and Karl Marx. *See also:* OBAMUNISM (p. 99).

Barat
(BAH-rat) *n.*

A Kazakh Obama supporter.

Baracademics

(buh-ROK-uh-dem-iks) *n.*

Obama's base. *See also:* OBALMA MATER (p. 73).

> Claims of Baracademic freedom have generally protected professors accused of actively stumping for Obama in the classroom.

Barackevorkians

(buh-ROK-eh-VOR-kee-ehns) *n.*

Those assisting with political suicide.

MEDIA

Baractopus

(buh-ROK-tuh-puhs) *n.*

A journalist capable of emitting vast quantities of ink relating to Barack Obama.

Barackumentary

(buh-ROK-yuh-MEN-tuh-ree) *n.*

YouTube.

Amabo Studios

(AHM-uh-boh) *n.*

Barack Obama's Chicago-based multimedia sister company to Oprah Winfrey's Harpo Productions.

Barack-and-bull story

n.

An absurd, improbable Obama story presented as the truth. *See also:* BARACKRYPHAL (p. 18).

Baracksploitation

(buh-RAK-sploi-TEY-shun) *n.*

The practice among editors of putting only Barack Obama on the cover of their magazines.

"It's like I was shot out of a cannon. I am so overexposed, I make Paris Hilton look like a recluse. . . . After all the attention—*People* magazine, *GQ*, *Vanity Fair*, Letterman—I figure there's nowhere to go from here but down. So tonight, I announce my retirement from the United States Senate. I had a good run."

Barack Obama at the 2004 Gridiron Club dinner

Barackryphal

(buh-ROK-ruh-fuhl) *adj.*

Of doubtful authenticity, in reference to a statement or story about Barack Obama. *See also:* BARACK-AND-BULL STORY (p. 16).

> Claims that Obama as a child attended a madrassa in Indonesia where he was schooled in radical Islamic teachings are largely Barackryphal.

Barackback Mountain

(buh-ROK-bak) *n.*

A depressing story of two cowboys unable to publicly express their sexual love for Barack Obama.

Barack to the Future

n.

A 2008 film in which Barack Obama uses the flux capacitor to defy traditional partisan politics, race, gender, and the space-time continuum.

Barackberry

(buh-RAK-ber-ee) *n.*

A means of staying in constant contact with all Barack Obama–related news.

> Despite attempts to ban the use of Barackberries during class, instructors have come to expect a chorus of chatter from the devices every time the campaign issues an alert.

Bar-echo chamber

(buh-REK-oh) *n.*

The comments sections on liberal blogs where Obamamaniacs reinforce one another's love for Obama and dislike of Hillary Clinton.

"Senator Obama, a minute ago Jorge Ramos asked you if there was anything we could get you and you said, quote, 'No thank you, I'm fine.' My question is, Are you sure? Because it's really no trouble."

Jason Sudeikis as CNN's John King on *Saturday Night Live*, February 23, 2008

SCIENCE

Baraxyribonucleic acid (BNA)
(buh-ROK-si-RAHY-boh-noo-KLEE-ik) *n.*

The molecules that, when introduced into ordinary human DNA, code for a deep, unwavering love of Barack Obama.

> Tom's support for Barack Obama was so stalwart, so fervent, that his friends wondered whether it found root in his very BNA.

Baracketology

(buh-ROK-eh-TOL-uh-jee) *n.*

The study of predicting how superdelegates will vote at the convention. Not to be confused with *Baracketry* (p. 26).

> Managers have discouraged office Baracketology for fear that discussion of superdelegate picks could bring all productivity to a halt.

Baracketry

(buh-ROK-i-tree) *n.*

The science of Barack design, development, and flight. Not to be confused with *Baracketology* (p. 25).

"Obama has a talent for extending forgiveness to the guilty and the anxious without requiring an apology from them first. Go forth and sin no more, he almost says, and never mind the reparations. No wonder they call him the brother from another planet."

Slate's **Jack Shafer**, "How Obama Does That Thing He Does," February 14, 2008

BaroxyContin

(buh-ROK-si-kan-tin) *n.*

A prescription painkiller sometimes abused by Obama supporters to induce feelings of euphoria while listening to Obama speak.

> While parents of younger Obama supporters tend to welcome their children's sudden interest in politics, rumors of BaroxyContin abuse at political rallies have given many cause for concern.

High Baractane

(hahy buh-ROK-teyn) *n.*

A theoretical fuel, made entirely from corn ethanol, that simultaneously ends pollution and saves American agriculture.

> Obama's proposal would require all new cars made in America to run on at least 85 percent high Baractane fuel by January 1, 2010.

Barackteria
(buh-rak-TEER-ee-uh) *n.*

A contagious single-celled microorganism through which Obamamania is spread. Contracted via stump speeches, rallies, and debates.

Hydrogen Baraxide
(HAHY-druh-juhn buh-ROK-sahyd) *n.*

A chemical compound that bleaches color and race from presidential politics.

Baraxygen

(buh-ROK-si-juhn) *n.*

A light element essential to survival for Obama devotees.

> Frequent incidents of light-headedness among Obama supporters at campaign rallies has forced aides to keep Baraxygen tanks on hand for emergencies.

Baracket scientist
(buh-ROK-it) *n.*

What one must be to understand the nuances of the nomination procedures.

Baracktorate
(buh-ROK-ter-it) *n.*

A PhD in Obamalogy. *See also:* BARACADEMICS (p. 11).

Frontal Obotomy

(FRUHN-tl oh-BOT-oh-mee) *n.*

A controversial surgery, used to relieve severe cases of Obamamania, in which essential nerve fibers in the brain are severed.

> After his frontal Obotomy, Frank's interest in posting Obama campaign material to his Facebook page dropped off dramatically.

Barametrak pressure

(bah-ru-MET-rak) *n.*

An atmosphere measure that, when too high, is capable of suppressing voter turnout for Obama on election night.

Obamamatic pilot

(oh-BAH-muh-MAH-tik) *n.*

An airborne control system that automatically directs a plane to the nearest campaign rally.

RELIGION

Deus ex Barachina
(DEY-uhs eks buh-ROK-ehn-uh) *n.*

The process whereby a papier-mâché Obama descends from the rafters to save humanity.

Obamageddon
(oh-BAH-muh-GED-n) *n.*

A fabled end of days predicted by supporters. Said to occur if Obama fails to win the election. *See also:* POST-BARACALYPTIC (p. 41).

"Democrats do have a historic race going. Hillary Clinton versus Barack Obama. Normally, when you see a black man or a woman president, an asteroid is about to hit the Statue of Liberty."

Jon Stewart, hosting the 2008 Academy Awards

Barack and tackle

(buh-ROK and TAK-uhl) *n.*

The ropes or chains and blocks used in hoisting Obama on and off stage.

> An otherwise well-executed town hall meeting hit a snag when the Barack and tackle that was to deliver Obama to the stage malfunctioned, leaving the candidate dangling several feet off the ground for the better part of a minute.

Post-Baracalyptic
(POHST-buh-ROK-uh-LIP-tik) *adj.*

Giving a harrowing glimpse of a hopeless future wherein Barack Obama is not elected president.
See also: OBAMAGEDDON (p. 38).

> The authors of the bestselling post-Baracalyptic novels have been accused of painting Big Hillary in an unnecessarily negative light.

Obamessiah

(oh-BAH-muh-SAYH-uh) *n.*

See BARACK OBAMA.

"Is Barack Obama—junior U.S. senator from Illinois, best-selling author, *Harvard Law Review* editor, *Men's Vogue* cover model, and 'exploratory' presidential candidate—the second coming of our Savior and our Redeemer, Prince of Peace and King of Kings, Jesus Christ? His press coverage suggests we can't dismiss this possibility out of hand."

Slate's **Timothy Noah**, "The Obama Messiah Watch," January 29, 2007

Dalai Lobama
(DAHL-ee loh-BAH-muh) *n.*

A religious and political leader who transcends partisanship through meditation from the Himalayas.

Barackolyte
(buh-RAK-uh-lahyt) *n.*

A devotee of the Dalai Lobama.

Obamukkah

(oh-BAH-muh-kuh) *n.*

An eight-day annual holiday celebrated by Obama supporters everywhere. *See also:* OBAMADAN (p. 46).

Barakmitzvah

(bah-rak-MITS-vuh) *n.*

A rite of passage for a young man in which he fulfills his duty of supporting Barack Obama.

Obamadan

(oh-BAH-muh-dahn) *n.*

A self-imposed fast by impoverished and overworked campaign workers.

Obamalisk

(oh-BAH-muh-lisk) *n.*

A four-sided pillar that loyal Obama supporters often construct in their backyards as a means of worship.

Baractrinate

(buh-ROK-truh-neyt) *v.*

To deluge a person with selections from the most recent Obama campaign press release.

> After only one semester away at school, Jen returned home thoroughly Baractrinated in the ways of Obama.

MUSIC

"Ob-la-di, O-ba-ma, life goes on"

n.

The opinion, infrequently expressed, that all is not lost if Obama fails to win the nomination.

Frère Baracka

(FRER buh-ROK-uh) *n.*

The protagonist of a campaign-themed French nursery rhyme.

"Obama Self"

(oh-BAH-muh SELF) *n*.

A tear-jerking cover of Eric Carmen's "All by Myself," to be released in the event Obama fails to receive the nomination.

Obamadeus

(oh-BAH-mah-DEY-uhs) *n.*

A young prodigy capable of composing oratorical masterpieces.

> Since Obama announced his candidacy, youth debating leagues have been overrun by parents who are convinced their child is the next Obamadeus.

New Kids on the Barack

n.

A source of campaign songs popular among nostalgic Gen-Y Democrats.

Baracturne

(buh-ROK-turn) *n.*

A sleepy, elegant song consisting of Barack Obama's voice accompanied by strings.

Barackenspiel

(buh-ROK-uhn-shpeel) *n.*

A musical instrument similar to a harp, famous for its heavy use in "Obama Self."

> Lifelong devotees of the Barackenspiel have expressed a certain cynicism concerning the instrument's sudden popularity.

Obambic pentameter

(oh-BAM-bik pen-TAM-i-ter) *n.*

The rhythm or cadence common in Obama's early experimentation with poetry.

"Barack-a-bye Baby"

(buh-ROK-uh-bahy BEY-bee) *n.*

What to sing to young voters to win their crucial support for Barack Obama.

Obamma Mia!

(oh-BAH-muh MEE-uh) *n.*

A musical based on Obama's life, with music by ABBA.

La Obamba

(LAH oh-BAM-bah) *n.*

A Spanish-language adaptation of *Obamma Mia!*

ANIMALS & CREATURES

Barackingbird
(buh-ROK-ing-burd) *n.*

A person who repeats Obama speeches and campaign material verbatim.

> Immediately after the release of the "Yes We Can" video, thousands of Obama supporters were temporarily transformed into Barackingbirds as they sang along.

Baracker spaniel

(buh-ROK-er SPAN-yuhl) *n.*

Any canine affixed with bumper stickers, pins, or other Obama campaign material.

Barackroach

(buh-ROK-rohch) *n.*

Barack Obama, as seen by supporters of Hillary Clinton.

> Rumors that the Barackroach is one of the few creatures that could survive a nuclear winter have been largely debunked.

Obaminable snowman

(oh-BOM-uh-nuh-buhl) *n.*

A legendary monster that stalks caucuses in Minnesota and Alaska.

Barack Ness monster

n.

A mythical seagoing creature spotted approximately once every four years. May be a fabrication of the media.

> News that the photograph of the Barack Ness monster circulating in the tabloids was a fraud did little to quell public belief in the creature.

Barachnid

(buh-RAK-nid) *n.*

A blogger who attempts, through an elaborate Web, to ensnare others into supporting Barack Obama.

Baracknophobia

(buh-RAK-nuh-FOH-bee-uh) *n.*

An abnormal fear of bloggers.

Baracking horse

(buh-ROK-ing) *n.*

A toy high horse, often made of wood, on which a young Barack Obama would compose stump speeches.

> Childhood friends recall that a young Obama would occasionally get on his Baracking horse and warn them against resorting to politics as usual on the playground.

Baracula

(buh-RAK-yuh-luh) *n.*

A batlike creature that feasts on the blood of moderate Republicans, turning them into Obama supporters.

Barackodile

(buh-ROK-uh-dahyl) *n.*

A leathery, cantankerous Obama supporter, largely made obsolete by the nullification of Florida primary results.

THE HYPE

Obomenon

(oh-BOM-uh-non) *n.*

See BARACK OBAMA. Synonyms: *Barackstar*, *Obamessiah*.

Barackstar

(buh-ROK-star) *n.*

A favorite nickname that thousands of supporters all believe they came up with themselves.

"He downplayed the fuss over his potential candidacy, saying he is just the flavor of the moment and a mere 'symbol or stand-in for a spirit that says we are looking for something different—something new.' It's wise for him to temper expectations for his candidacy. If voters stay in such a deep state of affection, they may get disappointed some day when he doesn't walk on water."

Slate's **John Dickerson**, "Following Obama through New Hampshire," December 11, 2006

Obamamania

(oh-BAH-mah-MEY-nee-uh) *n.*

A psychosis characterized by obsessive thoughts of Barack Obama.

> "I myself have been clinically diagnosed as an Obamamaniac, while my associate John King just last week suffered his third Barack attack." *Saturday Night Live*'s Kristen Wiig as CNN anchor Campbell Brown in a February 23, 2008, satire of the Democratic debates

Obamanation

(oh-BAH-mah-NEY-shun) *n.*

The United States the day after Obama's inauguration, when all strife and tension dissolve.

Obalma mater

(oh-BAHL-muh MAH-ter) *n.*

The place where one spent four years almost exclusively among Obama supporters. *See also* BARACADEMICS (p. 11).

Obamamatopoeia

(oh-BAH-muh-mat-uh-PEE-uh) *n.*

An excellent Barack Obama impression.

> While many took issue with *Saturday Night Live*'s choice of Fred Armisen to portray Obama, most agree that his Obamamatopoeia is spot-on.

Bamelot
(BAM-uh-lot) *n.*

An Obama White House styled after the Kennedy administration.

Barackadocio
(buh-ROK-uh-DOH-shee-oh) *n.*

The belief that one can win the general election based on a generic message of unity and change.

Obamalaise

(oh-BAH-ma-LEYZ) *n.*

The emotional hangover resulting from repeatedly listening to the "Yes We Can" montages.

Obamatose

(oh-BOM-uh-tohs) *adj.*

In a state of deep slumber, dreaming of Barack Obama.

Barackupied

(buh-ROK-yuh-pahyd) *adj.*

Unable to consider voting for any politician other than Obama.

"You hear this constant refrain from our critics that Democrats don't stand for anything. That's really unfair. We do stand for anything."

Barack Obama at the 2006 Gridiron Club dinner

Baracklamation

(buh-ROK-luh-MEY-shun) *n.*

Executive orders issued by President Obama.

Because Hope Awareness Day was established by a Baracklamation, it did not require the approval of Congress.

Barachismo

(buh-rak-EEZ-moh) *n.*

A strong sense that one's support for Obama confers moral authority.

> Ever since the Larsons planted an Obama sign in their yard, they've been carrying themselves with an exaggerated sense of Barachismo at parties and neighborhood events.

Obasm

(OH-baz-uhm) *n.*

The average reaction to an Obama speech. Often feigned.

Baroxysm

(bah-ROK-siz-uhm) *n.*

A sudden, violent spasm of affection for Barack Obama, often recurring periodically.

Barackturnal emission

(buh-rok-TUR-nal) *n.*

An ecstatic nocturnal reaction of Obama supporters.

Obamamentum

(oh-BAH-mah-MEN-tuhm) *n.*

A surge in poll numbers that generally follows a string of Obama primary victories. Not to be confused with *omentum*, a fatty wall of tissue in the abdomen.

STAND FOR CHANGE
CHANGE WE CAN BELIEVE IN
STAND FOR CHANGE
CHANGE WE CAN BELIEVE IN
CHANGE WE CAN BELIEVE IN
CHANGE WE CAN BELIEVE IN
CHANGE WE CAN BELIEVE IN

THE CAMPAIGN

BYOBama

(bee-wahy-oh-BAH-mah) *n.*

A grassroots campaigning method in which supporters are required to furnish their own campaign paraphernalia.

Obamiasma

(oh-BAH-mahy-AZ-muh) *n.*

The toxic atmosphere that lingers after a vitriolic Obama-Clinton debate.

"If anyone saw *Saturday Night Live*, you know, maybe we should ask Barack if he's comfortable and needs another pillow."

Hillary Clinton during the February 26, 2008, Democratic debate in Cleveland, Ohio

Barackheed Martin

(buh-ROK-heed MAHR-tn) *n.*

The company that manufactures attack ads for the Obama campaign.

Baracktagon

(buh-ROK-tuh-gon) *n.*

The Department of Defense headquarters once Obama adds three new wings.

Barackiavellian

(buh-RAK-ee-uh-VEL-ee-uhn) *adj.*

Describing a political strategy based on a recurring emphasis on unity and hope, as first laid out in Machiavelli's *The Obama*.

> While a by-the-book Barackiavellian approach to politics vaulted Obama to a national figure in the first months of his campaign, his advisers soon realized they would need more substantive policy proposals to sustain his popularity.

Obamerang

(oh-BAM-uh-rang) *n.*

The tendency for any criticism of Barack Obama to bounce back and result in one's resignation.

Operation Baracki Freedom

n.

An operation designed to liberate Americans from the yoke of partisan politics. May or may not provide adequate plans for reconstruction.

> While thousands of supporters have thrown their weight behind Operation Baracki Freedom, little is known about Obama's plans for reconstruction after the fall of politics as usual.

"We are bringing together Democrats and Independents and, yes, some Republicans. . . . An Obamacan, that's what we call 'em. They whisper to me, they say, 'Barack, I'm a Republican. But I support you.'"

Barack Obama, speaking in Madison, Wisconsin, February 12, 2008

Barack-paper-scissors

n.

A decision-making game that Obama will employ to choose his running mate.

> Obama's announcement of his vice president was delayed by a bitter fight among aides over whether Barack beats paper.

Baraxymoron

(buh-ROK-si-MAWR-on) *n.*

Any time a candidate simultaneously touts his or her experience while running on the theme of "change."

Barack exchange

n.

A building or other place where political allegiances are bought and sold.

Barawkward moment

(buh-RAWK-werd) *n.*

An uncomfortable exchange of forced pleasantries between candidates.

"You're likeable enough, Hillary."

Barack Obama at the January 5, 2008, debate in New Hampshire

96

Obameter

(oh-BOM-i-ter) *n.*

The counter on the Obama Web site that tracks donations.

Obautomated teller machine

(oh-BAW-tuh-meyt-id) *n.*

An electronic banking machine that accepts cash donations to the Obama campaign. Deposits only.

Baracketeering

(buh-RAK-i-TEER-ing) *n.*

The practice of offering superdelegates political "protection" in exchange for their support. *See also:* OBAMAFIOSO (p. 8).

> Senior Obama aides vigorously denied charges that their political donations to undeclared superdelegates amounted to Baracketeering.

Obamachine

(oh-BAH-muh-sheen) *n.*

The Obama campaign's Chicago field office.

Obamunism

(oh-BOM-yuh-niz-uhm) *n.*

The governing structure for the Obama campaign's volunteer network. *See also:* OBAMRADE (p. 10).

Barackracy

(buh-RAK-ruh-see) *n.*

A form of government in which Barack Obama has unlimited authority.

The cult of worship surrounding Barack Obama has led some to fear that his popularity and apparent immunity to political attacks will allow him to run his administration as a de facto Barackracy.

OBAMAMANIA!

Barackumen

(buh-RAK-yuh-muhn) *n.*

A shrewdness for navigating the campaign trail.

Obambidextrous

(oh-BAM-bi-DEK-struhs) *adj.*

Having the ability to hold one's Obama campaign sign for hours in either hand.

Barackadaisical

(buh-RAK-uh-DEY-zi-kuhl) *adj.*

Succumbing to the temptation among some Obama supporters to believe that nothing can halt Obama's momentum.

> Obama's sagging poll numbers throughout the summer of 2007 were proof of the danger of becoming Barackadaisical during the campaign.

PARAPHERNALIA

Obambrero

(oh-bom-BRAIR-oh) *n.*

A broad-brimmed hat of straw or felt affixed with campaign paraphernalia.

Barackenstocks

(buh-ROK-uhn-stoks) *n.*

Footwear unusually popular among Obama supporters. *See also:* BARACKCASINS (p. 107).

Barackcasins

(buh-ROK-uh-sins) *n.*

Heelless shoes made entirely of soft leather, useful for long hours of door-to-door canvassing.

Shoe retailers in the Des Moines area were warned to stock up on Barackcasins ahead of the influx of campaign volunteers on their way to Iowa.

Barackintosh

(buh-RAK-in-tosh) *n.*

A computer that is highly likely to identify the owner as an Obama supporter.

On a given Sunday afternoon, coffee shops in young, urban areas are invariably filled with Obama supporters updating their campaign profiles on their Barackintosh notebooks.

XBaracks 360

(eks-buh-ROKS) *n.*

An increasingly popular console featuring games in which the player emulates Barack Obama with a four-button controller.

> Critics have held that the popular XBaracks 360 is not teaching players real-life political skills.

Obamahawk

(oh-BOM-uh-hawk) *n.*

A light ax used by the Obama campaign's hatchet men.

> While Obama has done his best to distance himself from slash-and-burn politics, his campaign has its share of aides prepared to throw an Obamahawk into the Clinton machine if necessary.

Obarmulke

(oh-BAH-muhl-kuh) *n.*

A skullcap affixed with Obama campaign material often worn by Jewish supporters, particularly during Obamukkah.

FOOD & DRINK

Baracktoberfest

(buh-rok-TOH-ber-fest) *n.*

Beer-infused parties and rallies celebrating an Obama victory. *See also:* BARACCHANALIA (p. 115).

> The Obama campaign was forced to cancel Baracktoberfest when aides realized that over half their supporters could not legally consume alcohol.

Baracchanalia
(buh-RAK-uh-NEY-lee-uh) *n.*

Similar to Baracktoberfest, but featuring wine as the preferred beverage.

Baracklava
(buh-RAH-kluh-vah) *n.*

A sweet, nutty delicacy served at Obama rallies in Greek American neighborhoods.

Baracktail

(buh-ROK-teyl) *n.*

A mix of cheap liquor and Kool-Aid served during Baracktoberfest.

Baratwurst

(buh-ROT-wurst) *n.*

A short, thick sausage popular at before-rally tailgates.

Barackardi and Coke

(buh-rah-KAR-dee) *n.*

Another popular quaff during Baracktoberfest.

Political opponents charged that the Obama campaign's serving of Barackardi and Cokes on the day of the Puerto Rico primary was a tacit encouragement of voting under the influence.

Baraccoli

(buh-ROK-uh-lee) *n.*

Healthy alternative to Baratwurst.

"Eat your Baraccoli," a shorthand for the contemplation of the "hard truths" of Obama's message, proved to be an especially unpopular campaign slogan and was quickly shelved.

CONTRIBUTORS

Slate would like to thank the following people who suggested words for this book: Jennifer A. Bacher, Jeffrey Barton, Richard Beal, Gabrielle Bennett, Kiran Bhatraju, Seth Chalmer, Sean Crane, Russ Daly, Curtis Desilets, Lauren Dula, Jim Festante, John C. Fontana, Matthew Gasparich, Ted Getzel, Valerie Greear, Max Grover, Jonathan Gunderlach, Janis Hansell, Matt Heitner, David Hill, Travis Horseman, Chris Jansen, Nathan Jensen, Joe Jesselli, Harold Johnson, Rachel Johnston, Claire Beck Keeler, Jason Kinkle, Laura Kirwan, Stanley Marcus, Meghann McCormick, Mike McKinlay, Angela Miller, Joe Mitchell, Kevin Moriarty, David Muhammad Sr., Michael Myers, Timothy O'Brien, Scott Radnitz, Michael Sargent, Bill Smee, Luke Swanson, Spencer Toth, Daniel Viederman, Donald H. Wilkerson, Tom Wilson, Omar Yacoubi, Peter Yanke.

PHOTO CREDITS

Jahi Chikwendiu/ *The Washington Post*: viii, 104
Linda Davidson/"staff/ *The Washington Post*: 12,22,36,48,84
Gerald Martineau: 58
Melina Mara/ *The Washington Post*: 68
Rich Lipski: 112